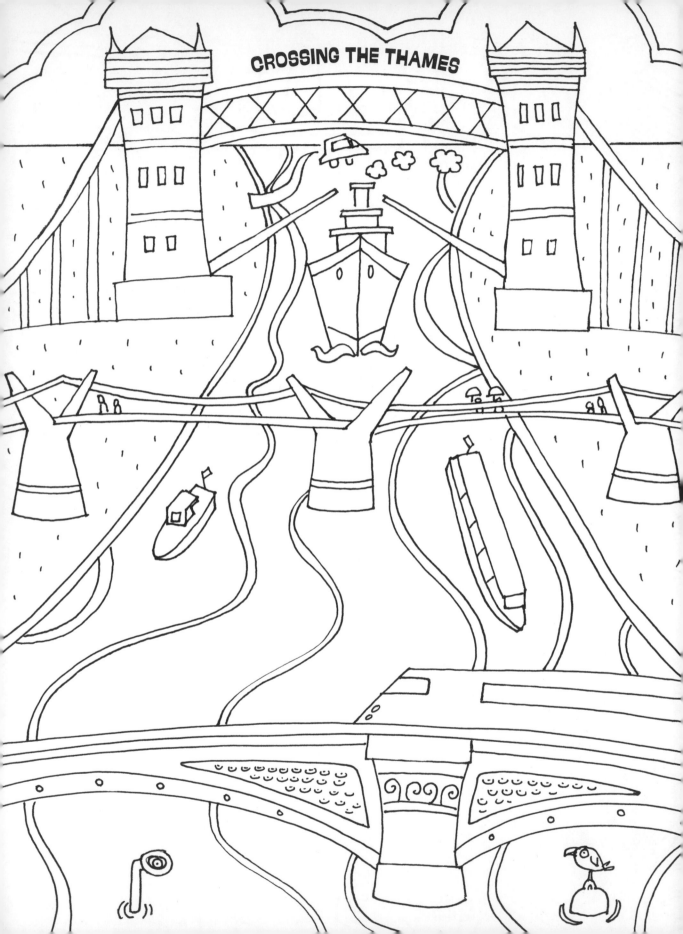

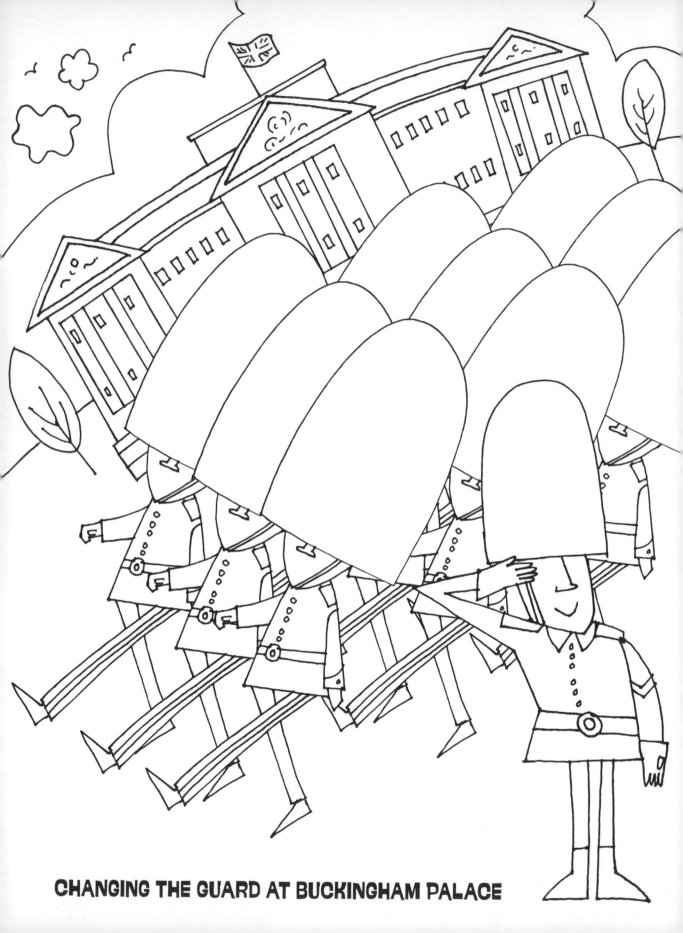

CHANGING THE GUARD AT BUCKINGHAM PALACE

REPTILES

AQUARIUM

NELSON'S COLUMN AT TRAFALGAR SQUARE

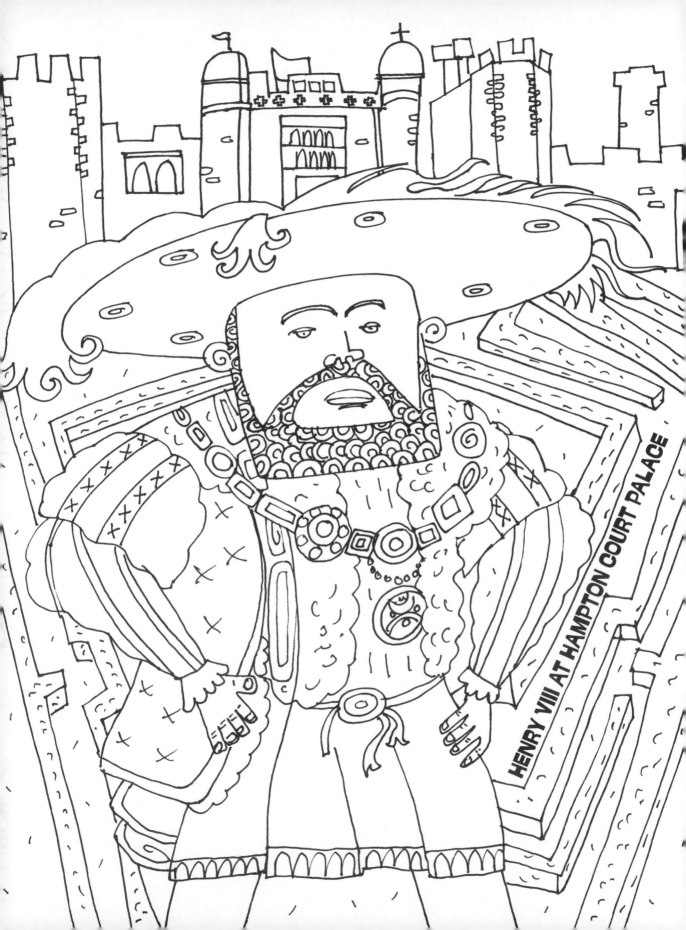

HENRY VIII AT HAMPTON COURT PALACE

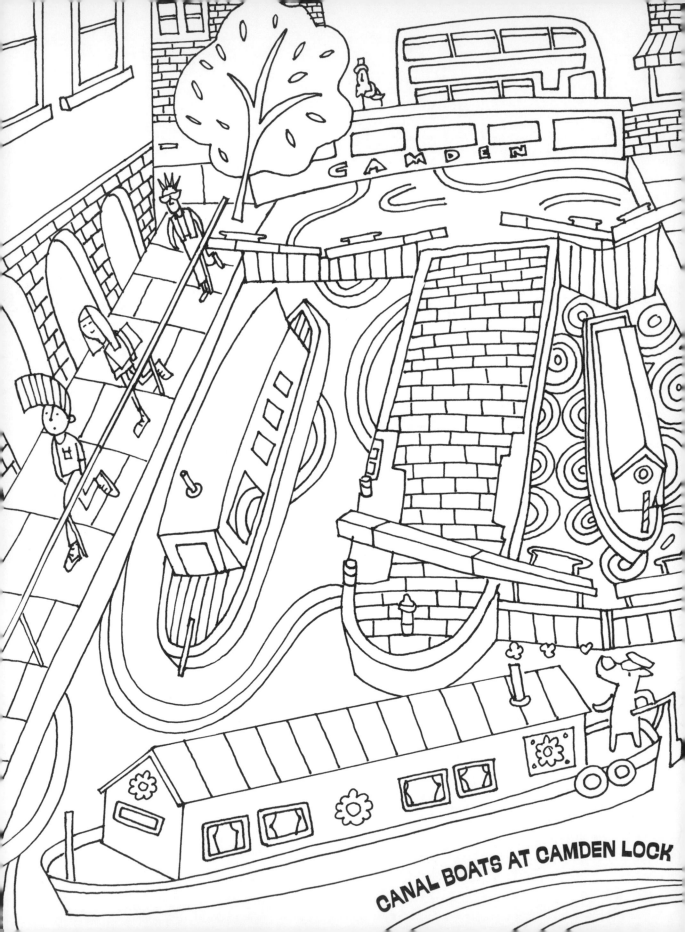

CANAL BOATS AT CAMDEN LOCK

SET SAIL ON THE SERPENTINE
IN HYDE PARK

MAKING WAVES AT WESTMINSTER

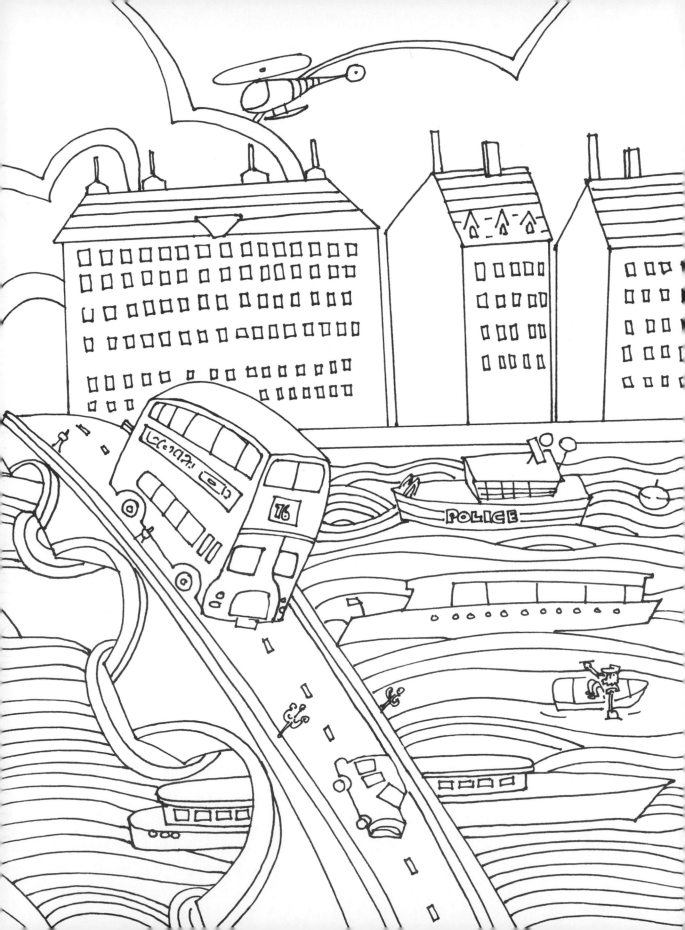

TROOPING THE COLOUR

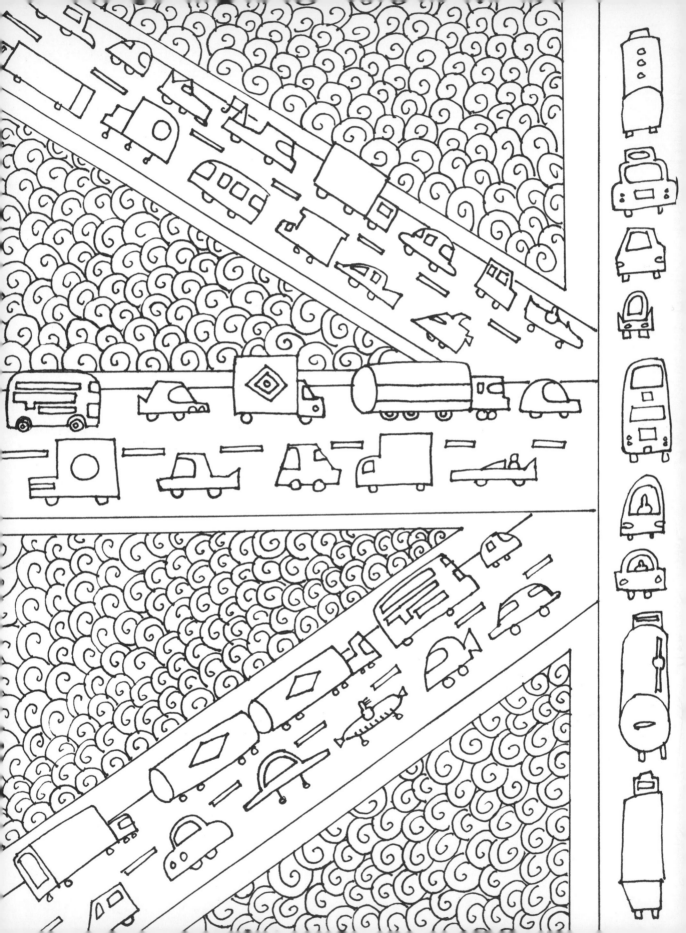

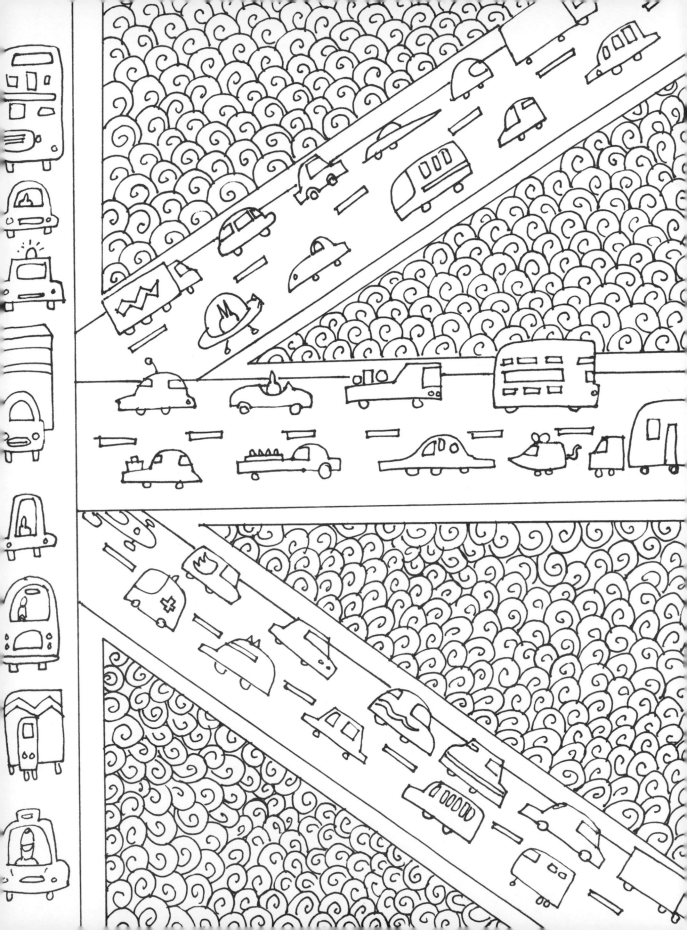

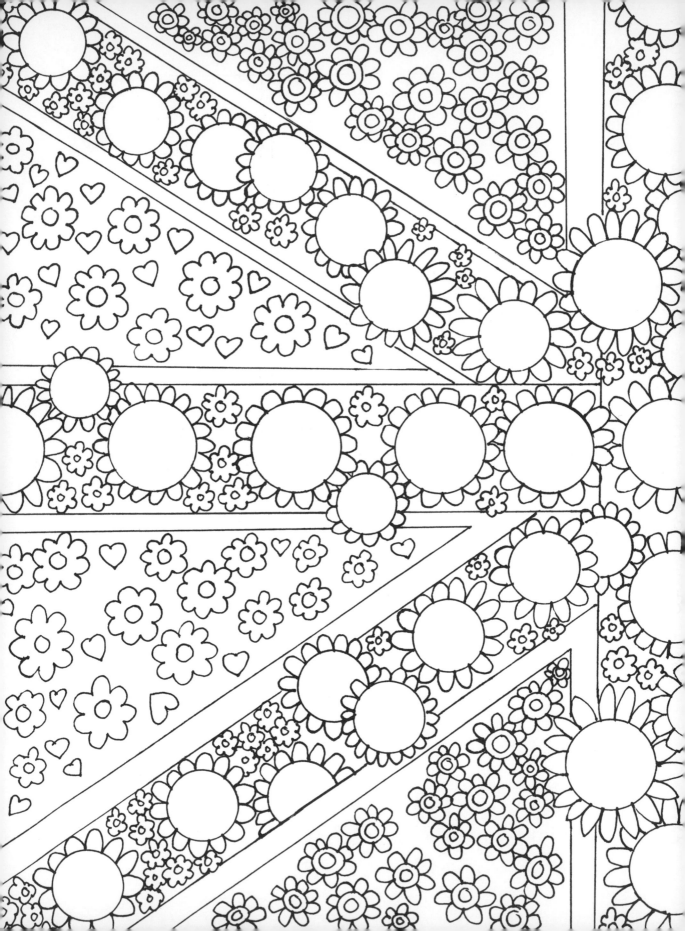

ST PAUL'S CATHEDRAL

THE MONUMENT TO THE GREAT FIRE

GOING FOR GOLD AT THE OLYMPIC PARK

THE PRINCESS OF WALES MEMORIAL FOUNTAIN

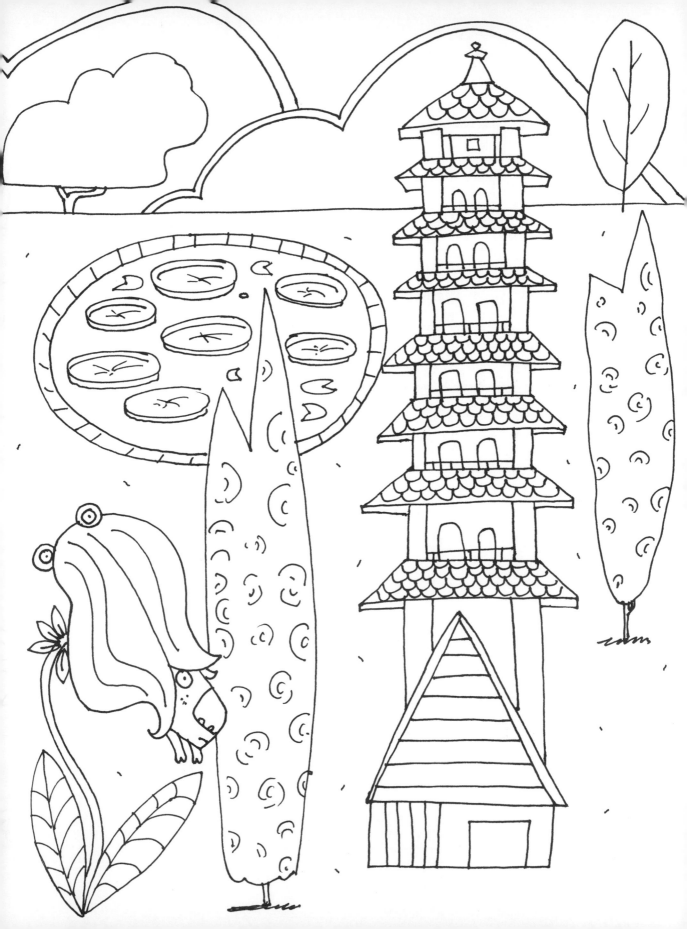

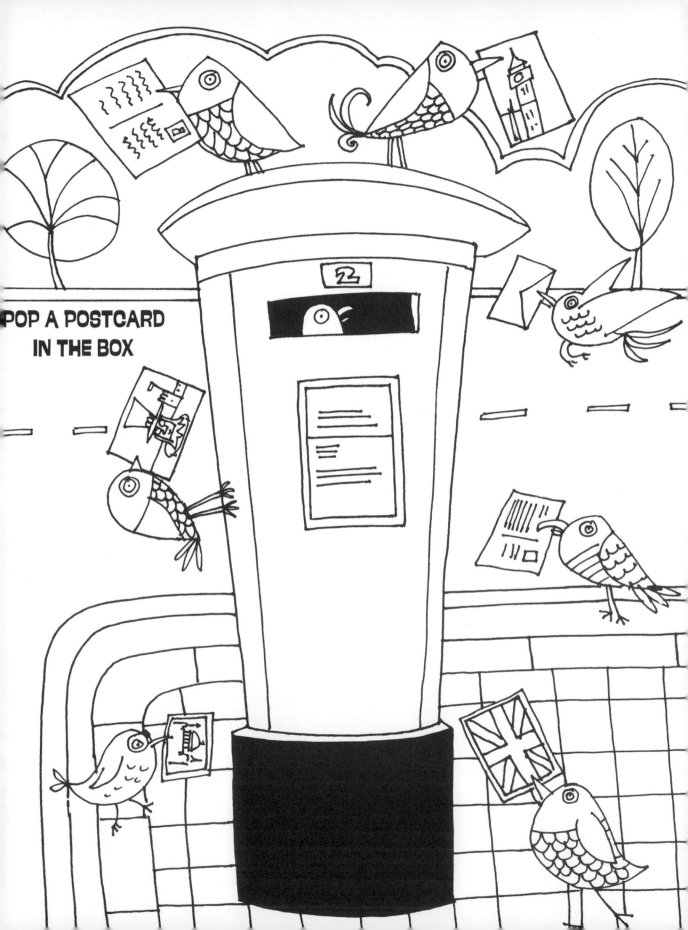

POP A POSTCARD
IN THE BOX

TAKE A PEEK AT THE CROWN JEWELS

EAST MEETS THE WEST END IN CHINA TOWN

First published in Great Britain in 2012 by Buster Books,
an imprint of Michael O'Mara Books Limited,
9 Lion Yard, Tremadoc Road, London SW4 7NQ

This revised edition was first published in 2024 by Buster Books.

W www.mombooks.com/buster

f Buster Books

 @BusterBooks

 @buster_books

A CIP catalogue record for this book is available from the British Library.

ISBN: 978-1-78055-980-3

1 3 5 7 9 10 8 6 4 2

This book was printed in November 2023 by
Leo Paper Products Ltd, Heshan Astros Printing Limited,
Xuantan Temple Industrial Zone, Gulao Town,
Heshan City, Guangdong Province, China.

MIX
Paper | Supporting
responsible forestry
FSC
www.fsc.org
FSC® C020056